Popstars

by **Linda Strachan**
illustrated by **Michael Reid**

Chapter One

There was going to be a show at school. Hope wanted to be in the show. So did Kamal and Beth.

Beth wanted to put on a play. Hope wanted to tell jokes. But Kamal didn't want to do that.

Kamal wanted to be in a pop group, like The Dragons.

They all liked The Dragons.
"We can be The Hut Dragons!"
said Kamal.

Beth wanted to sing. Hope was cross.

She wanted to sing, too.

Hope was cross. Kamal wanted her to come back.

Beth wanted Hope to come back too.

They could both sing.

Chapter Two

Nicky let Beth have his guitar. Dad let Kamal have his drums.

They all got dressed up.

They had a lot of fun.

Hope's mum came in. The girls were playing and singing. They were good.

“You are good,” said Mum.

“We can win this!” said Beth.

“Yes, we can win!” said Kamal.

Kamal wanted to ask The Dragons pop group to come to the show.

Kamal would not tell Hope what she was doing. What if The Dragons didn't want to come?

Chapter Three

It was the day of the show. Beth and Hope were dressed up...
but where was Kamal?

Mums and dads were coming for the show but Kamal was not there. Where was she?

Kamal ran up to Hope and Beth. She was back!

"What were you doing?" asked Hope.

"I can't tell you," said Kamal.

Now they were all dressed up. They started to sing. It was lots of fun.

The show was good.

"They liked it, Kamal!" shouted Hope.

But Kamal wasn't there!

"Where is Kamal?" said Beth.

Then Beth and Hope saw Kamal. She had The Dragons with her. They *had* come to the show!

Hope, Kamal and Beth got to sing with
The Dragons.

They had a lot of fun.

You were all very good but The Hut Dragons are the winners!